THE LIFEGUARD AND THE MERMAID

AND OTHER AMERICAN FABLES

FOUR SHORT PLAYS BY NORMAN DIETZ

Library of Congress Cataloging in Publication Data

Dietz, Norman D.
    The life guard and the mermaid.

    CONTENTS: The fun house mirror, a reflection.—The life guard and the mermaid.—The doll factory. [etc.]
    I. Title.
PS3554.I38L5   812'.5'4   75-38194
ISBN 0-8170-0702-4

Printed in the United States of America ⊕

For Sandra
who upstages me in all of them

— AND FOR FRED, WITH
THANKS FOR YOUR ENTHUSI-
ASTIC WORK IN MY "SHOP"
WARM REGARDS,

[signature]
PHOENIX
88

Plays by
NORMAN DIETZ

The Apple Bit
Old Ymir
Deus Ex Machinist
Tilly Tutweiler's Silly Trip to the Moon
Harry and the Angel
O To Be Living, O To Be Dying
The Life Guard and the Mermaid
The Doll Factory
The Phonebooth Fable
Noah Webster's Electrick Arktype
The Firemen's Picnic
Jesustory
Scenario For An Unmovie
I Used To See My Sister
The Well-Spoken Acrobat
Robinson Crusoe Eats It
Sonofthebeach
Le Drugstore
Millenimum

Collections of Plays

Fables & Vaudevilles & Plays: *Theatre More-Or-Less At Random,*
1968
The Life Guard and the Mermaid, *And Other American Fables,*
1976

CONTENTS

The Fun House Mirror: A Reflection 7

The Life Guard and the Mermaid 11

The Doll Factory 37

The Phonebooth Fable 48

Noah Webster's Electrick Arktype 61

The Fun House Mirror: A Reflection

Fables are paradigms of the human condition; simple stories, mostly, about extraordinary happenings. They are not really founded on fact (in truth, they are usually obvious lies); but they manage to be true anyway, by celebrating a mystery at the heart of existence.

At any rate, that is how *I,* a dyed-in-the-wool fable-maker, choose to define *mine;* and in the world of definitions, as in the world of fables (there being more than a little of each in the other), personal choice is everything.

My fables are also theatre pieces, of course: part play, part poem, and part tall tale. And that means, if you will endure another of my fable-maker's expositions, that like incorrigible children they ought rather to be heard than seen, to be spoken aloud and grasped in full flight by listening ears rather than scavenged by the solitary eye off pages in a book.

A good many of my fables, built as they are out of the common stuff of the comic stage—stock characters, jokes, puns, laugh lines and surprises—are also part two-a-day vaudeville. And I expect *that* is because I write them, first of all, for Sandra and me; and *we* like to laugh a lot.

Don't misunderstand. We approach the theatre, *and* my fables, with all the dignity and seriousness of purpose necessary to the proper celebration of great mysteries. It's just that great mysteries seem to make us laugh; they tend to strike us funny. And our dignity collapses.

We are something *less* than somber, in other words. Though we are not unmoved by the human predicament (on the contrary, of course, we are often moved to hilarity), our awe tends to be perverse; our celebrations tend toward the uproarious rather than the grave. We are not unquiet people exactly, nor giggling idiots *certainly;* and we worry, and we weep like other people. We are just ebullient much of the time, that's all; our spirits tend to bubble up and over. And in a theatre we are naturally *un*staid.

The theatre, it must be said, struck me long ago as being as good a place as any to house spirits such as ours, a better place than *many* I have tried since then. For one thing, laughers seem to have a natural affinity for its strange blend of truth and fiction, its tolerance of ambiguity. For another, the theatre is one last place where grownups can behave like children (and I value that). As a matter of fact, it is one last place where *children*—increasingly expected these days, it seems, to behave, not like children at all, but like small, bored grownups instead—can behave like children, *too.* It is a place (anyplace, if it comes to that) where we can play together with impunity, a place where we can wander in, say, "Let's pretend," and lie a little to each other to explore the truth.

For that is what we are really doing in our playing: exploring what *is,* exploring the reality of our being. For as we play, we give ourselves to one another in our make-believe; and in the giving and receiving, in responding to its pretense, yielding to impulse, we betray to one another—often with unaccustomed freedom, sometimes inadvertently, without intending to, without particularly *caring*—how we feel about life and its riddles, about being alive, about being human.

And what takes place is often something very close to *confession.* It is a way of saying, "Yes, yes, my life is like that." (Or, "No, no, it isn't.") Because in our play together we set up all sorts of complex, interconnected networks of communication—between actors and actors; between actors and audience; *even* between individual members of the audience itself—the entire enterprise focused on the stuff of life, the truth of the human condition, mysteries about ourselves that lie beyond our comprehension, seen reflected, as if accidentally, in a made-up looking glass of lies. And our play becomes a celebration—an exploration and a celebration of what it *means* to be alive in a riddle, what it means to *us* to be human.

And if, natural tragedians that we are, we laugh unexpectedly at what we see in the mirror, if we giggle or lose our self-composure and guffaw, then we are laughing, it seems to me, first of all because the mirror, like those in some old-fashioned fun house, is just slightly out of kilter; and the two-a-day vaudeville life we see reflected in it, and the outrageous postures we all assume in response, look suddenly, miraculously comic, instead of tragic as expected, the difference being obviously one only of definition after all, only of point of view, of changing one's way of looking.

What has happened is that we have been taken by surprise by a distortion; we have been gloriously ambushed by a cockeyed view of life (often even of what we find most evil and tragic) that makes us feel relief and release from it; a celebration of human reality, even of evil and tragedy, that seems at one and the same time mercifully to overlook our responsibility for its sad state while never for a moment allowing us to forget our complicity in its being.

How does the comic point of view do this? It makes the ridiculous laughable rather than tragic, it seems to me, because the comic perspective senses and communicates the sense that although human evil and the long shadow of tragedy that it casts over life are very grave matters indeed, still, from a different perspective, genuinely confronted and confessed, they don't really matter very much after all.

In this respect, comedy, I think, is a recognition of what the Christian churches have traditionally labeled *grace*—the feeling that an element, however nontheologically defined, of forgiveness, of unmerited and unanticipated forbearance, is at work in the universe; a certain cosmic sufferance of human life that long ago allowed it to begin and now, our suicidal pretensions to the superhuman notwithstanding, for a time at least allows it still.

Comedy is an *exercise* in this forgiveness; it is confession and absolution; it is a testimony to sufferance and forbearance made human and understandable—made effectively *active*—through incarnation in the humblest things of life. And if, as many people have pointed out, there is always an element of cruelty and violence in comedy, in the distorting mirror and its unflattering reflections, perhaps that is because there is always, necessarily, a large element of violence present in any act of forgiveness—a very intense, very personal violence—and a willing acceptance of it, resulting in release.

American audiences, of course, are not usually looking for this. Or we do not *think* that we are. We spend our time overturning stones and opening floating bottles in search of messages. We *worry* about messages; we have bad dreams about them, particularly those we fear we may have overlooked (though how anyone with a television set could overlook *many* these days somehow escapes me). We are obsessed with missing something, with missing the crucial information.

Well, I enjoy talking about my fables with audiences, but I am not really sure I *have* a message. I do not think I am in possession of any privileged information. I am therefore more interested in *meaning* than in *message,* in what *happens*—in the empathy, the laughter (and the tears) that come when people play together with genuineness; I am more interested in that immediate response to meaning, in that revelation of self, that openness and acceptance, that giving and receiving, than in any kind of intellectual analysis.

That, I suppose, is because for me, as a fable-maker, the mystery at the heart of existence remains bafflingly beyond my powers of definition, its fuzzy shape never more than dimly and momentarily illuminated by sudden half-deceptive flashes of revelation that leap out at me from, among other places, comic bits of good news written backward by some jokester on a fun house looking glass silvered with lies.

These are enough, however. They tell me I am not alone in the darkness and convince me that the Great Mystery at the heart of it, like most riddles, is benign. And my uproarious laughter at it all— embarrassingly loud, my wife informs me, though it is she most often who holds the silvered mirror—is only my giddy "Hallelujah!" in reply.

Orient, Long Island
September 15, 1975

The Life Guard and the Mermaid

A Fable for Two Players

THE LIFE GUARD AND THE MERMAID, sole occupants of this flimsy theatrical sand castle, are surrounded by a seashore teeming with people and crammed full of things—an unseen reality of great importance to the fable. It is therefore on the creation of this seaside world of sand, water, sunbathers, hamburgers, and guns (yes, guns; this is America), rather than on such traditional actors' concerns as character and motivation, that the players ought chiefly to concentrate. They should also keep the tone of the play buoyant and its pace brisk to save its weighty theme from possible death by drowning.

I wrote this piece during May and June of 1975 on commission from the American Baptist Churches in the U.S.A. Richard Jones of the ABC National Ministries staff, a man with nerves of steel surely, midwifed my labors. His understanding and willingness to experiment were limitless, as are my thanks to him. Sandra and I first performed the play on June 26 and 27 (we chopped it into two parts) at the ABC's Second Biennial Convention in Atlantic City, New Jersey. We had a ball.

THE LIFE GUARD AND THE MERMAID

[*A life guard and a mermaid—once upon a place, once upon a time.*]

LIFE GUARD   [*To the beach below, where the audience finds itself inadvertently sitting*] All right, bathers, this is your Life Guard speaking.

MERMAID   [*To him*] Excuse me.

LIFE GUARD   Clear the area for Emergency Life Saving Drill.

MERMAID   Could you tell me if this is where Big Sand Pile Island used to be?

LIFE GUARD   [*To her*] Lady, this *is* Big Sand Pile Island.

MERMAID   Really?

LIFE GUARD   Can't you read the sign on the hamburger stand?

MERMAID   I can't even *see* the hamburger stand.

LIFE GUARD   Welcome to the Club.

MERMAID   I beg your pardon?

LIFE GUARD   The Big Sand Pile Island Volunteer Life Saving Society and Private Beach and Sunbathing Club.

MERMAID   Oh.

LIFE GUARD   For *Members Only*.

MERMAID   My.

LIFE GUARD   This is *our* island, and that's our hamburger stand you can't see over there in our hamburger smoke.

MERMAID   [*Squinting but not seeing it*] Very nice.

LIFE GUARD   [*To the beach*] All Volunteer Life Savers report to the water and fall in immediately. [*To her*] Excuse me, I'm conducting Emergency Life Saving Drill.

MERMAID   I wouldn't have recognized it.

LIFE GUARD   Life Saving Drill?

MERMAID   No, Big Sand Pile Island.

LIFE GUARD   Oh.

MERMAID   It's so *small* to be *Big*.

LIFE GUARD	Well, it's been shrinking. Small but tall, we say, he-heheh. [*To the beach*] On the double down there!
MERMAID	What do you call this monstrosity we're standing on?
LIFE GUARD	[*To her*] This is our sand castle.
MERMAID	You don't say.
LIFE GUARD	Big Sand Pile Sand Castle, tallest sand castle in the Atlantic.
MERMAID	Wow.
LIFE GUARD	We figure the sun must be shining up here *some*place if only we can get up above the hamburger smoke and *find* it.
MERMAID	Sounds logical.
LIFE GUARD	You can see some of the Club Members down there right now with their little red and white sand pails, digging up that last bit of sand between the beach umbrellas and the hamburger crates.
MERMAID	Oh, yes.
LIFE GUARD	Meantime, it's a nice place for the Head Life Guard Post.
MERMAID	Oh, are you the Head Life Guard?
LIFE GUARD	Yes, Homer Beachcomber.
MERMAID	How do you do.
LIFE GUARD	[*To the beach*] All hands prepare for Life Saving Drill Number One.
MERMAID	My name is Ethel.
LIFE GUARD	[*To her*] Pleased to meetcha.
MERMAID	I'm a mermaid.

13

LIFE GUARD   Yeah, I could tell from the seaweed wig and the rubber tail.

MERMAID   I'm on official business.

LIFE GUARD   Me, too. Excuse me. [*To the beach*] Commence Life Saving. Ready . . . Aim . . . *Fire!*

MERMAID   Zowie!

LIFE GUARD   [*To her*] Pretty impressive, huh?

MERMAID   Yes, is that Life Saving?

LIFE GUARD   That's how we do it on Big Sand Pile Island.

MERMAID   Whose life does it save?

LIFE GUARD   Ours.

MERMAID   Oh.

LIFE GUARD   [*To the beach*] Reload and prepare for Drill Number Two.

MERMAID   Where do you aim?

LIFE GUARD   [*To her*] Out toward that sandbar you passed on your way in.

MERMAID   But that's full of *people*.

LIFE GUARD   That's why we aim at it.

MERMAID   Aren't you afraid you might hit them?

LIFE GUARD   Oh, gosh no. *They* are, but *we* aren't, heheheh. They're troublemakers.

MERMAID   They *seemed* harmless enough.

LIFE GUARD   They keep wading in through the hamburger smoke and sneaking up on our Private Beach.

MERMAID	Who could blame them? They're knee-deep in water out there every high tide.
LIFE GUARD	They're after our hamburgers.
MERMAID	Maybe they're hungry.
LIFE GUARD	No, they're failures, *that's* what they are. Lazy, good-for-nothing failures.
MERMAID	Where did they come from?
LIFE GUARD	Right here, can you beat it? They used to buy hamburgers down at the hamburger stand. Who'da thought they'd turn out to be hoodlums.
MERMAID	Were they Members?
LIFE GUARD	No, neighbors.
MERMAID	Oh.
LIFE GUARD	Greedy, high-living neighbors that used to sell us beach sand for our castle.
MERMAID	I see.
LIFE GUARD	We had a very nice arrangement: They sold us beach sand for our castle, and we sold them hamburgers for breakfast, lunch, and dinner.
MERMAID	Sounds fair enough.
LIFE GUARD	Heck, yes. We paid them a nickel a pailful.
MERMAID	What'd you charge for the burgers?
LIFE GUARD	Five bucks a throw. They're *good burgers.*
MERMAID	I *hope* so.
LIFE GUARD	Shoulda seen them dig, *wow!* This island used to be twelve miles across! And eat? *Boy!* You'da thought hamburgers were going outa style. Matter of fact,

they *did* go outa style. With all that digging and eating, three months ago they ran outa beach and hamburger money on the same day. So they all waded out to that sandbar and sat down. Actually, there wasn't much else they *could* do. Except sit down in *here,* of course, but that's against the rules. Life Saving Drill tends to keep them in their place. Except when the smoke gets extra bad. Serves them right, *I* say. Very poor planning on their part, very little economic foresight.

MERMAID   I'm not good at mathematics.

LIFE GUARD   Mermaids aren't expected to be.

MERMAID   That's not our business.

LIFE GUARD   No. What *is* your business, by the way?

MERMAID   I have a message for you.

LIFE GUARD   Really?

MERMAID   From Neptune.

LIFE GUARD   Neptune, New Jersey?

MERMAID   No, Neptune the Great. Neptune, the god of the sea.

LIFE GUARD   Is *he* still alive?

MERMAID   Yes, he is.

LIFE GUARD   What's his message?

MERMAID   "I'm gonna get you."

LIFE GUARD   Humnh?

MERMAID   "Woe unto you, Homer Beachcomber. Woe unto you, Big Sand Pile Island Volunteer Life Saving Society and Private Beach and Sunbathing Club. I'm gonna *get* you!"

LIFE GUARD	*Yeow!*
MERMAID	"I'm gonna *wipe you out!*"
LIFE GUARD	You *sure* Neptune said *that?*
MERMAID	Yes, he said, "I'm gonna send a tidal wave to swallow you."
LIFE GUARD	*A tidal wave!*
MERMAID	"Two hundred and twenty-three feet high."
LIFE GUARD	Cripes, what'd we *do?*
MERMAID	He says you stole his beach.
LIFE GUARD	His *what?*
MERMAID	His private beach.
LIFE GUARD	That beach was dry land.
MERMAID	It was his *seashore.*
LIFE GUARD	That's a technicality.
MERMAID	Neptune says you took it out of his sea while he wasn't looking.
LIFE GUARD	*We* didn't take his silly beach.
MERMAID	It's *missing.*
LIFE GUARD	It *is not,* it's right here. You're standing on it. It's just vertical instead of horizontal, that's all. We just relocated it.
MERMAID	Neptune liked it in the water.
LIFE GUARD	He's got water on the brain.
MERMAID	Well, he's out for blood right now. He says you're gonna pay for stealing his property.

LIFE GUARD	It's *not* his property, it's *ours,* we bought it. By the *bucketful.* We paid good money for it to those looneybirds out on the sandbar. You tell Neptune if he's out for blood, he can get it from *them.* Their blood is redder than ours anyway. I *see* it occasionally.
MERMAID	Blood is blood to Neptune. His eyes are bad. It all looks alike to him, especially in hamburger smoke. So long. Have a nice doom and destruction.
LIFE GUARD	Hey, wait a minute, *wait* a minute! *We* can settle *this.* Maybe we could take the castle *down,* how's that? We'll take the whole thing down and give the sand back.
MERMAID	Neptune doesn't want his sand back. He says you've defiled it.
LIFE GUARD	Oh. Well, how about hamburgers then? They're undefiled. Does he like hamburgers? Tell him we'll give him hamburgers, why not? We'll give him all he wants—thousands, *millions! With everything!* And lots of French fries on the side.
MERMAID	Hamburgers give Neptune indigestion.
LIFE GUARD	Hamburgers give everybody indigestion. People love them.
MERMAID	Neptune doesn't.
LIFE GUARD	Okay, we'll give him an interest in the business. What could be better, right? Fifty percent. *No,* seventy-five, what the *heck,* he's a *great guy!* We'll make a very attractive settlement.
MERMAID	Neptune doesn't make settlements. Neptune only makes waves.
LIFE GUARD	Okay, okay. No deals. We owe him for the beach, we know it. And it's our own darn fault, we admit it. We admit *everything.* We're thieves. It's true, we're miserable thieves. But we're sorry, see? We're

18

ashamed. We're overwhelmed with guilt and remorse. We cast ourselves on his mercy. Look, I fall on my knees. [*He does.*] Ooof. Tell him how sad and pitiful I look on my knees. *Plead* with him.

MERMAID   No, I'm sorry.

LIFE GUARD You won't tell him? You won't plead with him?

MERMAID   It's no *use,* the tide's turning already.

LIFE GUARD *Oh,* my gosh!

MERMAID   And the wind's blowing a gale out of the northeast.

LIFE GUARD Okay, *he* asked for it, Neptune *asked* for this.

MERMAID   What's the matter?

LIFE GUARD You're under arrest.

MERMAID   *I'm* under *arrest?*

LIFE GUARD This is a private club.

MERMAID   So what?

LIFE GUARD Are you a Member?

MERMAID   No.

LIFE GUARD Then you're under arrest.

MERMAID   For what?

LIFE GUARD Trespassing.

MERMAID   I'm not trespassing, I'm on official business.

LIFE GUARD [*To the beach*] Life Savers, man your guns!

MERMAID   Neptune is expecting me back.

LIFE GUARD [*To the beach*] Prepare to reverse Life Saving Drill!

MERMAID   I have to write a report.

LIFE GUARD [*To her*] Well, you can start by saying you were unavoidably detained.

MERMAID   You're a *beast!*

LIFE GUARD No, I'm Head Life Guard. And *you* are Miss Flood Insurance of 1976.

MERMAID   Neptune will get you, Homer.

LIFE GUARD Yes, and when he does, he'll get you, too, isn't that cozy? We'll all go together when we go.

MERMAID   It won't work.

LIFE GUARD Yes, it will.

MERMAID   I'm a mermaid, I can live underwater.

LIFE GUARD Yeah, but when Old Oysterguts starts playing sand castle upside-down cake with his tidal wave, you aren't gonna be underwater, honey, you're gonna be under*ground*. You're gonna be the first permanently installed mermaid on Big Sand Pile Island.

MERMAID   I'm a first-rate swimmer.

LIFE GUARD And a *marvelous* hostage, if I do say so myself. Just a *wonderful person* to have around! But if you don't want that pretty little seaweed wig of yours pushing up shoots out from under what was once Big Sand Pile Sand Castle, you better hope the Great Fish Eyes notices you missed the boat today and decides to see what happened. Because those idiots with the guns and spatulas down there are up to their you-know-whats in water. [*To the beach*] Hi, Club Members! Isn't it fun at the beach? [*To her*] I don't wanna spread panic. [*To the beach*] Attention, Life Savers. Give me your attention, kids. I have just been informed by an unimpeachable source close to the god of the sea that there is going to be a slightly high tide today, so we'll all have to take a few minor precautions, hahahah. So put down your guns, and stick your spatulas—uh, in your apron strings, and all hands heave to and round up those crates of stockpiled hamburgers, and start piling them up around the—*hey,* what's the matter here? Testing, one-two-three—[*To her*] Oh boy, the water's shorted out the public address system! [*Into the mike*] *Testing, one-two*—[*To her*] Wouldn't you *know!* I'll just have to yell. [*Yelling toward the beach*] Can you hear me down there? I said start stacking the hamburger crates against the *castle!* Did you *hear* me? Otherwise it'll wash away if there should possibly happen to be one very large wave or something, heheheh! Do you *read* me? *Do you read me! That's* right, the *crates* of *hamburgers, good! Fine!* That's the way! Just bring them all over *here* now! Keep up the good work!

MERMAID   You can't fight Neptune with hamburgers.

LIFE GUARD   [*To her*] Are you kidding? Those burgers're heavier than sin. [*To the beach*] Hey, what's going on down there? *Hey!* Life Savers! *Club Members!* Not over *there,* over *here!* Heheheh! Around the base of the *castle,* I said! The *castle! Cas-tel! C-A-S-T-E-L! Can you hear me?* [*To her*] My gosh, I'm yelling as loud as I can, and they can't seem to hear me.

MERMAID   I told you, you can't fight Neptune with hamburgers.

LIFE GUARD   [*To the beach*] *Over here, you nincompoops! Over here around the castle! CAS-TEL!* [*To her*] What a time to lose power! [*To the beach*] Don't you dummies understand English? What're you *doing* down there?

MERMAID   It looks like they're building a castle, a funny-looking little castle out of hamburger crates.

LIFE GUARD   [*To her*] My gosh, they *are!* That's what they're *doing!* They're making their own castle and crawling up on top of it to get out of the water.

MERMAID   And look who's coming *now!*

LIFE GUARD   Those bean bags from the *sandbar!* They're wading in toward the hamburgers and waving their fists.

MERMAID   [*Turning from the sight and hiding her face*] I can't watch.

LIFE GUARD   [*To the beach*] Attention, Life Savers! Nonmembers at twelve o'clock! Nonmembers closing rapidly at twelve o'clock!

MERMAID   What's happening?

LIFE GUARD   [*To her*] They're grabbing the hamburger crates and ripping apart the castle. They're also grabbing the Club Members and trying to rip *them* apart.

MERMAID   Oh, no!

LIFE GUARD   They're all splashing around in the water, fighting over the hamburger crates, and now they're pulling the Life Savers' helmets off, and I can't tell who's who, but they're all punching and pulling in the water, and the water's almost up to their necks now, and some of the crates are breaking open, and there are hamburgers *everywhere!*

MERMAID   I can't bear to look!

LIFE GUARD   And now everybody's stopped fighting, and everybody's just scrambling every which way after the hamburgers, and everybody's dragging hamburger crates all over the place, and now the water's rising over their heads, and some of them are *going under!*

MERMAID   [*Turning to him*] *Save* them, Homer, *save* them! *You're* the *Life Guard!*

LIFE GUARD   *How* can I save them? I can't find my *gun!* And who would I *shoot?* I can't tell them *apart!* Wait! *Look!* They don't *need* me! They're all climbing back up on top of the crates as if they were little islands, and now they're all just sitting down up there, each one on his own little crate, dripping wet, just staring across the water at each other, chewing their hamburgers. [*The*

MERMAID is staring, too, now.] And somebody's *pointing* at something, see? Look over *there*. He's looking out to sea and *pointing!*

MERMAID   *Everybody's* looking out to sea! They're *cheering!*

LIFE GUARD   [*To the beach*] What's the matter, everybody? What's going *on* down there? Why are you cheering? [*To her*] They're all yelling up at us, but I can't hear a word they're saying.

MERMAID   I think the water's stopped rising.

LIFE GUARD   Humnh?

MERMAID   The gale has shifted into the west. Look, it's blowing the flag on the flagpole straight out. And the tide has stopped flowing.

LIFE GUARD   Yes, it has! By golly, it *has!* See? Didn't I *tell* you? We've *stopped Neptune!* We've stopped Neptune *dead in his tracks!* You're a *marvelous* hostage!

23

MERMAID   Thanks. Can I go now?

LIFE GUARD   Of course you can't go now. As soon as you go, the wind shifts, and in comes the tide again. Nothing doing.

MERMAID   What do you suggest?

LIFE GUARD   Permanent residence. Honorary Club Membership, heheheh. How would you like to be Assistant Life Guard?

MERMAID   I'd rather die.

LIFE GUARD   Don't be dramatic.

MERMAID   [*Getting teary-eyed*] And if you keep me here past sunset, that's exactly what I'll do.

LIFE GUARD   Whaddya mean?

MERMAID	I'll die.
LIFE GUARD	You're kidding.
MERMAID	Mermaids only live for a day.
LIFE GUARD	I thought you lived forever.
MERMAID	Only underwater.
LIFE GUARD	*Oh,* my God!
MERMAID	[*Batting tearful eyes up at him*] Out in the air we wither like flowers and fade with the sunlight at dying of day.
LIFE GUARD	Oh, brother!
MERMAID	It's Neptune's truth.
LIFE GUARD	It's a trick. And I don't believe it.
MERMAID	You've got to.
LIFE GUARD	Yeah? How do I know you're not lying?
MERMAID	[*Miss Innocence*] You just have to trust me.
LIFE GUARD	Oh, sure.
MERMAID	But you have to, you *have* to! *Please! Don't* make me die! I don't want to *die!*
LIFE GUARD	Well, neither do *I,* for pete's sake! And if I let you swim off, I probably *will. Very promptly!*
MERMAID	Please.
LIFE GUARD	I'll only be sorry.
MERMAID	Please!
LIFE GUARD	I'm not gonna be a sucker for a mermaid.

MERMAID   *Please!*

LIFE GUARD   No!

MERMAID   *Please!* [*She sobs.*]

LIFE GUARD   Oh . . . All right! Go on! Get out of here! *Quick!*
               Before you turn my stomach!

MERMAID   [*Immediately recovered and leaving posthaste*]
               Thank you, Homer. I'll always remember you. [*She
               dives into the water, with style naturally.*]

LIFE GUARD   Bull! [*Watching her swim away*] Well, there she
               goes. So much for life insurance. There goes the
               wind into the northeast. [*With a glance at the flag
               above him*] Yep. [*And another at the beach*] And
               here comes the tide again, I knew it, I *knew* it! It's
               lapping at the bottom of the *castle* now! It's washing
               away the sand in the foundation! [*To the sea*] That's
               not fair, Neptune! That's not *fair,* do you *hear* me? I
               just did a good deed, Neptune! What'sa matter—
               don't you count *good deeds* any more?

                                                                          25

MERMAID   [*Sounding far away*] Tough luck, Homer.

LIFE GUARD   You shut your mouth, Ethel!

MERMAID   Goodbye, Homer.

LIFE GUARD   [*Giving her the raspberries*] Blurrrbbbbbbbbb! [*To
               himself*] Some lousy life. Try to do something
               constructive, and the whole world hates you. Do a
               little good turn, and nobody even cares. End up like
               a piece of driftwood at high tide. [*Shouting out to
               sea again*] Is that any way to run an ocean? I hope
               you swallow a *fish,* Ethel! Did you *hear* me? I said
               next time you open your big fat mouth, I hope you
               swallow a *fish!* And I hope you *choke* on it!

MERMAID   [*Immediately, at his side again*] Excuse me.

LIFE GUARD   [*Without even looking*] Oh no, not *again.*

MERMAID   Can we talk?

LIFE GUARD   I thought we just finished.

MERMAID   We did, but I'm back.

LIFE GUARD   Not by popular demand, I can tell you. Back from
              where?

MERMAID   From the bottom of the sea.

LIFE GUARD   Well, I think you lost your equipment in the rush.

MERMAID   Excuse me?

LIFE GUARD   Where's the seaweed wig and the rubber tail?

MERMAID   I've got good news for you.

LIFE GUARD   That's all I need—a little more good news from you.
              Any more good news from you, I jump off the
              castle and *kill* myself. I'd be better off dead.

MERMAID   That's what I came to *tell* you.

LIFE GUARD   I'd be better off dead?

MERMAID   No, there's gonna be a slight delay.

LIFE GUARD   In what?

MERMAID   Your doom and destruction.

LIFE GUARD   Humnh?

MERMAID   The water's stopped rising again.

LIFE GUARD   Not *again!* Can't you undersea beings make up your
              wet little minds?

MERMAID   But that's *good* news, isn't it? Look! For the first
              time in twenty years the sun is peeking through the
              hamburger smoke. [*To the beach*] Chin up, flood
              victims, the worst is over! Chin up, down there! [*To

him] They can't *hear* me, of course, but the important thing is to look confident and keep up their spirits. [*To the beach*] Three cheers for the gallant inhabitants of the Hamburger Islands!

LIFE GUARD   What're you *doing?*

MERMAID   [*To him*] I'm being encouraging. [*Waving and smiling toward the beach*] Wave and look confident.

LIFE GUARD   I wanna die.

MERMAID   [*Turning back to him*] Why? You've got everything to live for.

LIFE GUARD   What have I got? A big pile of sand that's washing away.

MERMAID   It's a *castle.*

LIFE GUARD   It is *not.* In the hamburger smoke it may have *looked* like a castle, but in the sunlight, believe me, it's a *pile.* I'm gonna jump.

MERMAID   But you're the Head Life Guard.

LIFE GUARD   Okay, I'll do a swan dive. Stop interfering. Go back to the bottom of the sea where you belong.

MERMAID   I *can't* go back there.

LIFE GUARD   Why?

MERMAID   I'm not a mermaid anymore.

LIFE GUARD   Why not?

MERMAID   I quit.

LIFE GUARD   Are you outa your mind?

MERMAID   Almost. I was a mermaid for a *million* years. It nearly drove me *crazy!*

LIFE GUARD   Why?

MERMAID   It bored me!

LIFE GUARD   Listen, the best jobs in the world're the ones that're most boring.

MERMAID   Oh, yeah?

LIFE GUARD   Sure. It usually means you don't have much to do.

MERMAID   *I'll* say! All *I* ever got to do was announce *dooms*.

LIFE GUARD   Well, that's better than *suffering* them, hahahah.

MERMAID   But I said to myself a zillion times there must be a better way to spend your life than just announcing *dooms.*

LIFE GUARD   I used to feel that way about Life Saving Drill.

MERMAID   Only I could never figure out what it was that might be better.

LIFE GUARD   I know the feeling.

MERMAID   So I'd just go out and announce my dooms as politely as I could and then swim away into the sunset and fill out my reports. It was pretty dull stuff, but the pay was good, and the hours were nice. And Neptune always said just stick to your swimming and announce your dooms and don't get *funny ideas.*

LIFE GUARD   [*Shrugging and nodding*] Umnh.

MERMAID   *Besides,* I never really knew what a doom *was* anyway. I never really stuck around before to see one *happen.* Then this afternoon, of course, *wow!* Did *yours* ever make an *impression!*

LIFE GUARD   Yeah, it made an impression on me, too.

MERMAID   And as I swam off into the sunset, I got to thinking.

And all of a sudden, I wished I *hadn't*. Because suddenly it struck me that maybe I *shouldn't* have because maybe you could use a little *help,* you *know?*

LIFE GUARD   [*Nodding*] I *know.*

MERMAID   Except *gosh,* how on earth does a *mermaid* help a *human?* I mean, *wow!*

LIFE GUARD   [*Shrugging and nodding*] Umnh.

MERMAID   I mean Neptune says flat out you *can't.*

LIFE GUARD   [*Dully*] Ahhh.

MERMAID   Yeah, Neptune says humans are *beyond* help. Neptune says, "The silly ninnies only go and *die* on you *anyway,* so what can you *do?*"

LIFE GUARD   He's got a point.

MERMAID   Yeah, but *I* don't think I *believe* that, you *know?* Because how does *he* know? I mean Neptune's not a *human,* he's a *god.*

LIFE GUARD   [*Shrugging*] Wull, yeah.

MERMAID   And *I* think if you're gonna *help* a human, maybe you gotta *be* one, because otherwise, how can you even *know* for sure if you *can?*

LIFE GUARD   Sonofagun!

MERMAID   So I decided maybe the thing for *me* to do was to *stop* this silly half-and-half-split-personality-being-a-*mermaid* thing and become a *person* instead.

LIFE GUARD   You don't *mean* it.

MERMAID   *Yes!* A real, live, whole human being *just like you!*

LIFE GUARD   I'll be darned.

MERMAID   So I made up my mind *right then,* and I swam up to

Neptune, and I said, *"Hey,* I'm *finished* with this *mermaid* stuff. I'm *sick* of doom and gloom, I wanna be a *woman!"*

LIFE GUARD   Wow!

MERMAID   As if all of a sudden I was working for someone *else,* you *know?* As if all of a sudden some strange *new* god from someplace *else* was scooping me up off the bottom of the sea and giving me this funny new *job!*

LIFE GUARD   What'd *Neptune* say?

MERMAID   He didn't say a *thing,* I couldn't *believe* it.

LIFE GUARD   Huh.

MERMAID   He's got this huge old wheel down at the bottom of the ocean with these great big paddles that he turns to make the wind and waves and tides and things?

LIFE GUARD   Yeah.

MERMAID   And he was turning this thing *lickety-split,* because it takes a *heck* of a lot of turning to make a two hundred-twenty-three-foot *tidal* wave.

LIFE GUARD   I'm not surprised.

MERMAID   And I just said, "Neptune, I don't think this mermaid stuff's *enough.* I wanna be a *woman.* Where do I hand in my seaweed wig and my rubber tail?"

LIFE GUARD   Boy, when you say it, you say it.

MERMAID   Yeah, you shoulda seen the look on his *face.* He turned *sea green!*

LIFE GUARD   I don't doubt it.

MERMAID   And these great big *bubbles* came out of his *ears,* and he just stopped turning his wheel and turned around and *stared* at me as if he couldn't believe what he was hearing.

LIFE GUARD   He probably couldn't.

MERMAID   He didn't roar, he didn't sputter, he didn't fume. He just *stopped* and *stood* there, half-bent over, with his hands on the handle, looking as if he might *never* start turning it *again.* I guess nobody ever said anything like that to him before.

LIFE GUARD   Probably not.

MERMAID   Well, I was just about to ask him what a mermaid had to *do* to *qualify* to be a woman when suddenly I started to feel all these really great, weird new *things* going on *inside* me, and I figured, *gosh,* all you have to do is *decide,* by golly. But then all at once I started to get *dizzy* and *short of breath,* and suddenly I realized I was scared to *death* I was gonna *die!*

LIFE GUARD   I know what you mean.

MERMAID   And it came to me that what you *really* have to do to become a human is decide not to *care!* Because there's so *doggone* many *human* things you just can't *do* without *dying,* and who really wants to be *eternal anyway?*

LIFE GUARD   [*Shrugging*] Wull, *I* dunno.

MERMAID   So I *shot* back up to the surface and *whizzed* over *here!* I lost my tail on the *sandbar,* and my wig flipped off in the *shallows* as I waded up on shore. But *here I am—Ethel the Human,* standing on my own *two feet!* Whaddya think?

LIFE GUARD   You were a rotten mermaid, Ethel. But as a person . . . you're not bad.

MERMAID   Thanks, Homer.

LIFE GUARD   But what do we do now?

MERMAID   Life Saving!

LIFE GUARD	Humnh?
MERMAID	Life Saving. I wanna do *Life Saving!*
LIFE GUARD	Oh, come on. I *told* you, Ethel, I *lost* my *gun.*
MERMAID	Not *that* kind of Life Saving.
LIFE GUARD	What other kind *is* there?
MERMAID	I wanna rescue those poor helpless creatures down there on the hamburger crates. I wanna get them up outa the water and keep them from drowning.
LIFE GUARD	Oh.
MERMAID	Isn't that a good idea?
LIFE GUARD	Yeah, but you can't call it Life Saving. The Board of Directors wouldn't stand for it.
MERMAID	Here's what we'll do. We'll jump in, swim out there, and bring them back here to the castle.
LIFE GUARD	Wait a minute. For one awful second I thought you said "we," hahahah.
MERMAID	I did.
LIFE GUARD	"We?"
MERMAID	Yes.
LIFE GUARD	*W-E, we?*
MERMAID	Yes.
LIFE GUARD	Is there somebody up here I can't see?
MERMAID	I don't think so.
LIFE GUARD	Then you *can't* mean *"we."*
MERMAID	Why not?

LIFE GUARD   I could *drown* in there.

MERMAID   Not if you swim.

LIFE GUARD   *Who* can swim? I'm afraid of the water.

MERMAID   But it's simple. I'll teach you.

LIFE GUARD   No, you won't.

MERMAID   Yes, I will. Just lie on your belly, paddle like a doggie, and wiggle your little rubber tail.

LIFE GUARD   I don't *have* a rubber tail.

MERMAID   Oh.

LIFE GUARD   And neither do *you.*

MERMAID   Gee, I wonder what we do.

LIFE GUARD   Stay here, I think. I think we stay here.

MERMAID   I suppose we kick our legs.

LIFE GUARD   *Suppose?*

MERMAID   We'll just have to jump in and find out.

LIFE GUARD   *Jump in and find out!*

MERMAID   Doesn't that sound logical?

LIFE GUARD   *No,* it sounds *dangerous. Very dangerous!* And that's not the only thing that does.

MERMAID   What do you mean?

LIFE GUARD   What if the guy I wiggle up to doesn't happen to be a Member of the Club?

MERMAID   Well, I'd say rescue him anyway. He can always join when he gets here.

LIFE GUARD	Yeah, but what if he doesn't *want* to?
MERMAID	Why wouldn't he want to?
LIFE GUARD	Well, the Volunteer Life Savers have been shooting at those dodos on the sandbar for three months now. What if I'm dogpaddling up with a smile of reconciliation on my face, and one of those peabrains hits me over the *head?* What if one of those knuckleheads grabs me by the ears and holds me *underwater?* I don't *breathe* too good that way.
MERMAID	They won't do *that,* you're coming to *rescue* them.
LIFE GUARD	Yeah, but who's gonna tell *them?*
MERMAID	You're coming with *love* in your heart.
LIFE GUARD	Sure, *I* know that, and *you* know that, but do *they* know it?
MERMAID	They'll see it shining in your eyes.
LIFE GUARD	Yeah, but they'll start belting me with hamburgers while I'm forty yards away. My eyes don't *shine* that far. Listen, maybe we should wait till the public address system's fixed. Maybe I could make a general announcement.
MERMAID	You can't explain love over a public address system.
LIFE GUARD	I could give it the old Beach Club try.
MERMAID	You've got to say it face-to-face.
LIFE GUARD	In *twelve* feet of *water?*
MERMAID	You've got to *reach out.*
LIFE GUARD	Can I sneak up from the *rear?* I could *hit* them over the head, *knock* them out cold, and then explain about the *love* bit when I got them *tied up* back here.
MERMAID	That's not the way a human treats a human.

LIFE GUARD   I can see you haven't been a human very long.

MERMAID   Don't *worry* so much.

LIFE GUARD   Who's worried? I'm *paralyzed with fear!*

MERMAID   Something will come to you in the moment of crisis.

LIFE GUARD   Yeah, sudden death.

MERMAID   I'll *help* you. I'll *stick close.* I'll *teach* you.

LIFE GUARD   But will you give me a decent *burial?*

MERMAID   Just hold your nose and jump on the count of three.

LIFE GUARD   Can I ask one question?

MERMAID   What's that?

LIFE GUARD   What about that tidal wave? Remember?

MERMAID   What about it?

LIFE GUARD   How long before it comes?

MERMAID   Well, that *depends.*

LIFE GUARD   On what?

MERMAID   On Neptune, naturally. On when he recovers from the shock.

LIFE GUARD   Oh, yeah.

MERMAID   He *could* snap out of it any minute.

LIFE GUARD   That's what I was afraid of.

MERMAID   Then again, he's very old now, and he may just stay there leaning on his wheel for a long, *long* time.

LIFE GUARD   But how will we *know?*

MERMAID   We'll listen to the weather reports.

LIFE GUARD   Everybody talks about Neptune, but nobody ever *does* anything about him.

MERMAID   Look at it this way: He hasn't stirred *yet!*

LIFE GUARD   No, but the *wind's* picked up a little, and the *waves're* getting bigger, and the *castle's* kinda crumbling around the *edges,* and I was wondering— what happens when we get all those people down there *up here,* and suddenly *up here* slides back *down there* and disappears?

MERMAID   We'll all do a lot more swimming.

LIFE GUARD   You're telling *me.* Where *to,* though?

MERMAID   What's beyond the horizon?

LIFE GUARD   How should *I* know? Nothing. *Water* probably.

MERMAID   Umnh, but you never know.

LIFE GUARD   No, you never know. Isn't that a *problem?*

MERMAID   *Heavens,* no! Who *cares?* The water's *fine!* Jump in and *swim* with me! [*To the beach*] Stand by for Life Saving Drill Number Three!

LIFE GUARD   I'll never be able to explain this to the Board of Directors.

MERMAID   Ready?

LIFE GUARD   Lie on my belly, paddle like a doggie, and wiggle my little rubber legs.

MERMAID   Right. One . . . two . . . three . . . [*A split second pause as she looks at him and he shrugs. And then, as she speaks, blackout.*] Ju-u-u-m-m-m-m-m-p!

[*And they are.*]

END

The Doll Factory

A Fable for Three Players

THE DOLL FACTORY is a theatrical grab bag full of clichés.
Dolly is that traditional, American eye-popper, the "dumb blond": a
coy, smiling, overendowed "innocent" with a breathy voice, long
golden tresses (probably phony), generous padding (probably ditto),
and legs that go, as a friend of mine used to put it, "all the way up to
her (location deleted)." Polly is the all-American drudge, an
overworked and, alas, underendowed homemaking machine. As a
result of heavy use and infrequent overhaul, her face is sagging, her

back is aching, her bottom is spreading, and her hair is beyond
control (but eternally set in plastic rollers). She talks loudly and
stares at the world as though she were expecting the TV to go on any
minute. Al American is a simple cross (but a heavy one) between a
high school principal and one of those guys who sells fireworks or
bedspreads at stands along highways. Written in June, 1974, on
commission from the Lutheran Church in America for presentation
before its 1974 National Convention in Baltimore, the play was
thought "too biting" and never actually produced.

THE DOLL FACTORY

[*The stage of the Al American Doll Factory auditorium. Three
chairs, and a podium perhaps, flowers and/or palms here and
there, and possibly bunting, too, or crepe paper decorations—all
the things most people use to clutter up a graduation. Amid the
clutter, two women and one man: Little Dolly Darling and Little
Polly Plain Jane, two of the dolls in this year's Al American
graduating class; and that little old dollmaker himself, Al
American, presiding at the ceremony.*]

DOLLY   Hi, I'm Little Dolly Darling. Welcome to the Annual
            Graduation Exercises here at the Al American Old
            Traditional Mass Production Doll Factory. Speaking
            for all the wonderful dolls in this year's class, I'd like to
            thank you for joining us for this important moment in
            our lives and introduce the man behind the machines
            here at the Doll Factory, our maker, Mister Al
            American himself. [*She applauds.*]

AL   Thank you, Little Dolly Darling. Thanks, folks. Isn't
            she a beautiful thing? You don't find a doll like that in
            every factory, do you? No, siree!

DOLLY   Oh, Al American, you're something else! [*To POLLY*]
            Isn't Al American something else?

POLLY   Yeah.

AL   It's the truth, Little Dolly Darling. Well, it's commence-
            ment time again, everybody, and before we get on with
            the festivities, I'd like to tell you how proud we all are of
            each and every one of the dolls who are graduating here
            today. They're as fine a bunch of dolls as ever left a
            factory.

DOLLY &
POLLY   Oh, Al American!

AL   And a real tribute to the wisdom and foresight of the
            American family and all the self-made men in it that
            drew up the patterns, made all the machines, and got
            the whole system going here at the Doll Factory away
            back in the good old days. Now, we don't produce a big
            variety of dolls here at Al American, and some people
            fault us for that, of course. We make mainly two models
            here, as you know: the low-priced regular and the high-
            priced luxury, always have and always will. Plus a few
            do-it-yourself customizing kits naturally, so's those who
            want low-priced regulars that ain't just run-of-the-mill
            can doctor up the trim a little and make 'em sporty or
            religious or intellectual or whatnot, *you* know; we do
            have them kits. And *one* thing we *always* do here at Al
            American: we make well-behaved dolls, and we make
            one heck of a lot of 'em. Yes, sir, real good old-fashioned

dolls, ain't that right?

DOLLY &
POLLY   That's right, Al American.

AL   All machine-made from the old tried and true patterns,
           guaranteed not to chip, crack, fade, peel, or get outa
           hand. Real old Al American dolls who know they're
           dolls and're proud of it because they believe in the Al
           American way.

DOLLY &
POLLY   That's right, Al American.

AL   Well, now, we don't have time to introduce all the dolls
           to you today. Mostly we'll just shake their hands and
           give 'em their Al American diplomas, *you* know. All
           them low-priced regulars look alike anyways. But we do
           want you to meet the cream of the crop, so to speak,
           those that've won special honors in their respective
           categories, dolls whose wonderful warm personalities
           and really terrible grades've earned 'em this year's Al
           American outstanding achievement awards. First, the
           doll whose laughing eyes and happy smile, whose silky
           blond hair and *terrific* figure place her indisputably at
           the head of her class; and whose amazing performance
           in this year's checkbook balancing contest won her the
           National Accountants' Citation as Financial Bust of the
           Year—here she is, the Class Valedictorian, our own
           Little Dolly Darling. [*He applauds.*]

DOLLY   Oh, thank you, Al American. Ave atque vale! Whatever
           that means. [*Giggles*] Hi, everybody! Gosh, what can I
           say? I mean, that we can all understand? [*Giggles*] We
           did it! [*Giggles*] Yes, we actually *did* it! Well, no,
           actually, *we* didn't do it, of course. I mean we're just
           silly little dolls, right?

POLLY   Yeah.

DOLLY   Al American *did* it, yes, he *did!* That wonderful, strong
           Al American and his great big wonderful machines.
           Oooh! [*Giggles*] I mean, how could any of us be
           anything but gorgeous and wonderful after what we been

through here?

POLLY   Yeah.

DOLLY   I mean the things we *learned!* Shorthand and cooking and sewing.

POLLY   Yeah, and baby care, don't forget baby care.

DOLLY   You go to your classes, honey, and I'll go to mine. [*Giggles*] I mean, we all had to skip *something, right,* Al American?

AL   That's right, Little Dolly Darling. Baby care is low-priced regular.

DOLLY   You're telling me.

POLLY   [*Shrugging*] I thought it was interesting.

DOLLY   Anyway, it's all over *now!* [*Giggles*]

40

POLLY   Yeah.

DOLLY   In a couple of minutes we'll be getting our diplomas and leaving the old Doll Factory in the dust.

POLLY   Yeah.

DOLLY   It'll be "Goodbye, Al American" and "Hello, Daddy!" Isn't it exciting?

POLLY   Yeah.

DOLLY   I mean, just think, cocktail parties and hair appointments and shopping trips and luncheons and charity dances—the real world at last! I can hardly wait to get a suntan. [*Giggles*] So long, everybody, see you in the toy store! [*Giggles*]

AL   [*Applauding*] Thank you, Little Dolly Darling. That was a wonderful speech, wasn't it folks? I mean, that's class for you, isn't it? Wow! [*Handing DOLLY a diploma*] Congratulations, Little Dolly Darling.

DOLLY   Thank you, Al American. [*She walks to her chair.*]

AL   [*As she walks*] Little Dolly Darling, ladies and
         gentlemen, the all-plastic plaything with the twenty-
         one-jewel movement, the doll that shows you earn
         enough to own the very best. Comes complete with a
         starter set of three wigs, thirteen costume changes, and a
         hundred thirty-seven pairs of shoes. All parts guaran-
         teed not to spread, shift, sag, or shrivel.

DOLLY & [*Singing and doing a little tap routine*] Hello, Dolly.
POLLY   Well, hello, Dolly. It's so nice—

AL   [*Interrupting*] Thank you, class. Next, representing the
         famous Al American Budget Division, a doll with a
         heck of a nice personality—and whose loyalty,
         trustworthiness, and perseverence make up for a lot—
         the winner of the Budget Division's Annual Popularity
         Contest, named by toy store owners the Doll Most
         Likely to Sell Out, Cheap, this year's Queen of the Low-
         Price Regulars—uh, what *is* your name, honey?

POLLY   Little Polly Plain Jane, Al American.

AL   Right. Little Polly Plain Jane, everybody. [*Aside to her*]
         Read your speech, honey.

POLLY   OK, Al American. [*She clears her throat, then reads
         with difficulty.*] Dear friends, esteemed manufacturer,
         and fellow dolls. [*She clears her throat again.*] I am not
         a very good—[*Trying to read it*] uh, writer. [*Looking
         up*] Or reader, hahah. [*Back to the page*] But Al
         American says as long as you can answer the phone and
         count to ten, it's OK. Al American says just cook a nice
         frozen dinner and try to look sexy, even if you just
         spilled hot canned tomato soup all down your front and
         the kid is screaming under the sink. Good old Al
         American, he knows a lot. He says just stick to your
         knitting and clean out the toilet good and make sure the
         guy gets the TV fixed before supper. Al American is my
         favorite manufacturer. He is a smart cookie. He makes
         a lot of money, but he doesn't have to give us a penny.
         Isn't that smart? Al American, we salute you. [*She does
         and then holds the salute.*] You are just like a husband
         to us.

AL   Uh, thank you, Little Polly Whatchamacallit. [*He
                  applauds, but less than enthusiastically.*]

POLLY   Plain Jane, sir.

AL   Plain Jane, right. [*Noticing she is still saluting*] At ease.
                  [*POLLY stops saluting.*] Not exactly your Little Dolly
                  Einstein, of course. But then, you can't have everything,
                  and we're not all millionaires anyway, are we? Heheheh.
                  And, of course, if you're looking for good old-fashioned
                  economy and durability, let's face it, Little Polly Plain
                  Jane can't be beat. [*POLLY smiles proudly.*] Well,
                  actually, she *can* be beat, but it won't do much *good*. Or
                  harm either for that matter.

POLLY   Oh, gosh no!

AL   Because Little Polly Plain Jane is built to last, made
                  outa bouncy sponge rubber with a sturdy cast iron
                  frame that'll stand up under years of rough treatment.
                  And topped off with a genuine, old-fashioned, stuffed-
                  sawdust head, guaranteed to go soft around the edges
                  just like mother's did.

POLLY   [*Grinning*] Yeah.

AL   Little Polly Plain Jane is designed to fit all standard
                  kitchens, laundries, and supermarket checkout coun-
                  ters. Factory-dressed in a simple cotton frock and
                  delivered complete with mouse-brown hair and six
                  dozen rollers. A few pregnant models, left over from
                  last year, available at half-price. [*Handing POLLY her
                  diploma*] Congratulations, Little Polly Plain Jane.

POLLY   You mean I finally passed, Al American?

AL   [*Aside to her*] Don't ask stupid questions, just take the
                  diploma.

POLLY   Thanks, Al American.

AL   You're welcome, I'm sure.

DOLLY   Does that mean we're graduated?

AL   That's right, Little Dolly Darling.

DOLLY   Wow!

POLLY   Yeah.

AL   That's it. Commencement's over for another year. Another great class leaves the old Doll Factory behind and walks out into the world of their dreams.

POLLY   Yeah.

DOLLY   Wow!

AL   But before we bring a halt to this year's festivities, I got a couple questions I always ask the Honor Dolls each year, and I'm sure we all wanna hear what this year's top award winners have to say, too. Little Dolly Darling, what're you gonna do now that you're graduated?

DOLLY   Oh, golly, Al American, I'm gonna be a famous model and meet a very rich man and buy lots of clothes and jewels and things and travel all over the world.

AL   [*Applauding*] That's wonderful, Little Dolly Darling. Isn't that wonderful, folks? Little Polly Plain Jane, what about you?

POLLY   Oh, I guess I'll just go to church. And have babies. Not necessarily in that order.

AL   [*Applauding politely*] Very nice, Little Polly Plain Jane.

POLLY   I make wonderful pork and beans, you know.

AL   Is that right?

POLLY   Yeah, that's a real crowd-pleaser.

AL   Certainly is.

POLLY   Especially if you got a really big pot.

43

AL   Yes.

POLLY   I feel if you got a big pot, there's always a place for you at church.

AL   Absolutely.

POLLY   But what I really wanna do is drive a bulldozer.

AL   Humnh?

POLLY   A bulldozer.

DOLLY   Little Polly Plain Jane!

POLLY   Yeah, I really wanna drive a bulldozer or a backhoe or a road grader!

DOLLY   Wow!

POLLY   I wanna sit up there behind the wheel in the sun with my shirt off and smoke a big cigar!

AL   But that's indecent!

POLLY   OK, I'll smoke a corncob pipe.

DOLLY   Oh, Little Polly Plain Jane, how exciting!

POLLY   Well, gosh, Little Dolly Darling, why don't you try it, too?

DOLLY   Oh, Al American, *can* I? Can *I* smoke a corncob pipe, *too?*

AL   It's not very doll-like, Little Dolly Darling.

DOLLY   Oh, I don't *care,* Al American, I wanna smoke a corncob pipe, *too!* [*Giggles*] I *do!* I wanna drive *all* over town in a white Cadillac convertible with the top down, puffing this *big* corncob pipe and *blowing* the *horn!* [*Giggles*]

AL   But, Little Dolly Darling—

DOLLY   I wanna scare a policeman!

AL   You can't *do* that!

DOLLY   Yes I can, I'll say, "Stand at attention, Sergeant, I'm your new police commissioner." [*Giggles*]

POLLY   *That'll* scare him.

AL   Hey, what's the matter with you two?

DOLLY   I'm gonna be a big politician and scare the whole *world!*

AL   I think you got a little manufacturing defect, Little Dolly Darling.

DOLLY   I don't care, I'm gonna be a powerful executive and run a big multinational corporation.

AL   [*To the audience*] It must be the machines, there must be something wrong with the machines.

POLLY   Yeah, *I'm* gonna be a famous boxer.

AL   Not you, *too!*

POLLY   *I'm* gonna play *pro football!*

AL   It's worse than I *thought!*

DOLLY   I'm gonna learn to play *poker!*

AL   Oh, no!

POLLY   *I'm* gonna study *plumbing!*

AL   It's a disaster!

DOLLY   *I'm* gonna be a fireman and sleep in my *underwear!*

AL   Somebody's ruined the machines! Some idiot's been tinkering with the patterns and fouled up the *machines!*

POLLY   *I'm* gonna join the Boy Scouts.

DOLLY   *I'm* gonna run for mayor.

POLLY   *I'm* gonna pump gas.

DOLLY   *I'm* gonna sing bass.

POLLY   *I'm* gonna go to the *men's room!*

AL   Stop! *Stop!* Stop the *machinery!*

DOLLY   Oh, Al American, isn't it *wonderful?*

AL   No, it's terrible!

POLLY   What'sa matter?

AL   You're dolls, that's what's the matter—*dolls!* Al American *dolls!* [*He salutes.*] First in war, first in peace, and first in the hearts of your countrypersons!

DOLLY   Well, so *what?*

AL   Dolls don't *do* things like that!

POLLY   Yes, we do.

AL   But you're not *supposed* to, that's the *trouble!* It's not in the specifications!

DOLLY   [*Proudly*] We do things other dolls *don't.*

AL   Yeah, but who wants a broad that's a mayor? Tell me, who wants a chick that lays sewer pipe and calls herself Fred?

POLLY   What else can we *do,* Al American?

AL   Be a librarian! Teach kindergarten!

DOLLY & POLLY & AL   [*Together*] Stick to your knitting and clean out the toilet and make sure the TV gets fixed before supper!

POLLY   For*get* it.

DOLLY   So long, Al American.

AL   You got a great future ahead of you!

POLLY   Thanks for the manufacture, Al American. [*DOLLY and POLLY exit.*]

AL   [*Calling after them*] Hey, what'sa matter? Come *back* here! You can't leave *now*, you got *defects!* You got serious *defects!* I'm recalling you, you *dummies;* you come *back* here! You got warped personalities! You got *flaws* in your *marbles!* You wanna walk around your whole life long with flaws in your *marbles?* Whaddya think you are—*people?* What'll the *customers* say? *Tell* me, what'll they *say,* huh? [*He turns back to the crowd.*] They don't care. They don't *care.* I think success went to their heads. Huh! [*A pause*] Well, like I said—that's the old Doll Factory graduation for this year. Hahahah. As you pass out, the ushers'll be at the doors as usual with order blanks and catalogues and a big graduation-sale supply of this year's top selling Old Traditional Tried and True Al American Dolls, every one of 'em a luxury or low-budget winner made by the *very same* machines as Little Dolly Darling and Little Polly Plain Jane, all packed up, as always, in fancy souvenir boxes and—uh, reduced for quick sale. Pick up a couple on your way home. There's a nifty little graduation surprise in every package.

END

47

The Phonebooth Fable

A Fable for Two Players

THE PHONEBOOTH FABLE was born on the Fifth Avenue bus in Manhattan during the summer of 1970. In working on the dialogue of another short play, ROBINSON CRUSOE EATS IT, I stumbled on five lines about living in a phonebooth and was so struck by the aptness of this familiar urban fixture as a symbol for life in the contemporary American environment that, before I left the bus, I had made a note of the idea and written the first few lines. I roughed out the piece, an exploration of the implications of the phonebooth metaphor, that summer—both in Central Park, where Sandra and I went to escape our apartment, and in the air-conditioned bedroom of our apartment, where we finally retreated to escape the stifling, yellowish-tan air of summertime New York. I had finished most of the fable by September when, yielding to feelings of urban doom, we decided to leave the city and move to the country. Its first performance was two years later in September, 1972.

In slightly different form the piece was published in 1975 in THE CHRISTIAN CENTURY.

THE PHONEBOOTH FABLE

SHE   Once there was a man who lived all alone in a phonebooth.

HE   "Hello!" he would say to the telephone on the wall. "I'm a man who lives all alone in a phonebooth."

SHE   For the phonebooth meant the world to him, and he liked to keep in touch.

HE   "Hello?" he would say

SHE   And lean close to the phone.

HE   "Hello, hello?"

SHE   But the telephone never answered.

HE   In thirty-nine years there wasn't a ring or wrong number.

SHE   Only dial tones and busy signals and occasional recorded announcements giving the time or the weather

HE   And now and then instructions to hang up and dial again.

SHE   He always did.

HE   "A man's phonebooth is his castle," he would say if you asked. "And one does what one can."

SHE   But, of course, no one asked.

HE   For he searched the directory from cover to cover thirty-nine times in his thirty-nine years

SHE   And he never found a familiar name to call.

HE   "Familiarity is a rarity in a phonebooth," he would say.

SHE   And so he spent his days dialing numbers at random and waiting for someone to answer.

HE   "Hello, I'm a man who lives all alone in a phonebooth," he would say when someone did. "How would you like to get familiar?"

SHE   *Click!* the telephone on the other end of the line would go.

HE   "Hello, hello?"

SHE   And so it went from day to day.

HE   "The telephone is a wonderful invention," the man would say. "But some days it is not exactly a million laughs."

SHE   Then suddenly one day everything changed.

HE   "Today is my fortieth birthday," said the man. "And also Friday the Thirteenth. And I think that's an omen."

SHE   For the phonebooth was a storehouse of tradition.

HE   "I feel that today laughter will enter my life."

SHE   And so it did.

HE   For just then, for the very first time, the man's telephone rang.

SHE   "Hello!" said a woman on the other end of the line. "I'm calling for Life."

HE   "Hello!" said the man. "I'm answering for a man who lives all alone in a phonebooth."

SHE   "Give yourself The Gift of a Lifetime!" said the woman.

HE   "I beg your pardon?" said the man.

SHE   "Put a little Life in your booth."

HE   "You're kidding," said the man.

SHE   "Life is full of excitement."

HE   "Life is out of existence, and I cannot subscribe to it."

SHE   "Well, it's your funeral."

HE   "No, technically, it's my birthday."

SHE   *Click!* went the telephone on the other end of the line.

HE   "Life is not what it used to be," said the man. "In fact, today it is not exactly even *one* laugh."

SHE   And hoping to forget, he bent down to try to tie his shoelace, which had come undone in the excitement.

HE   "In spite of Life," he said, "one can't allow oneself to come undone."

SHE But at that moment his telephone rang again, insistently.

HE "Happy birthday!" said the man to himself, still working on his shoelace.

SHE And it took him a short while to answer.

HE For it is no easy task for a man to bend down and tie his shoelace in a phonebooth.

SHE And it is even less easy for him to stand upright again.

HE "Hello!" said the man at last

SHE A little out of breath.

HE "I'm a forty-year-old man who has just been trying to tie his shoelace in a phonebooth."

SHE "Hello!" said a voice on the other end of the line. "This is God."

HE "Humnh?" said the man.

SHE "God. *You* know, from Sunday school, *remember?*"

HE "Oh, *yes!* How *are* you? We kind of lost track."

SHE "Yes, I've been looking for you."

HE "Well, I've been right here in the phonebooth."

SHE "Your *line* has been busy."

HE "Well, that's *Life,* I guess."

SHE "I beg your pardon?"

HE "Never*mind,*" said the man. "It's hard to explain."

SHE "Well, happy birthday, anyway! I've got good news for you."

HE "Really?"

SHE   "Yes, get a pencil and paper, and write this all down, because it's very important."

HE   "Okay," said the man.

SHE   And he got out his very best mechanical pencil with the five colored leads

HE   And a pad of fifteen sheets of clean new paper.

SHE   And he tucked the receiver between his chin and his shoulder.

HE   And he looked up at the light in the phonebooth ceiling

SHE   Half expecting it to be on

HE   Although he knew it had never worked.

SHE   And he began suddenly to feel very young.

HE   "Good old God!" he said to himself.

SHE   And he wrote

HE   "GOOD NEWS"

SHE   In capital letters at the top of the first page.

HE   "Okay, I'm ready!" he said as he wrote. "I'm ready!"

SHE   But there wasn't any answer.

HE   "God?"

SHE   Just a steady hum, and once some funny noises that went *burr-beep*.

HE   "Hello? Hello?"

SHE   But God was gone, just like that.

HE   "Gosh!" said the man. "Whatever happened to good old God?"

SHE   And he called Information.

HE   "Information?"

SHE   "Information is not what it used to be. This is Directory Assistance."

HE   "Oh. Well, I'm a man who lives all alone in a phonebooth."

SHE   "Good for you."

HE   "Listen, I was just talking to a friend of mine, and we were cut off, and I'd like to call him back, but I don't know his number, and I wonder if you could help me out?"

SHE   "With whom did you wish to *speak,* sir?"

HE   "God."

SHE   "I beg your pardon?"

HE   "G-O-D."

SHE   "I'm *sorry,* we do not have a *listing* for Mister God."

HE   "But we were just *talking.*"

SHE   "What *number* were you *calling?*"

HE   "I wasn't calling *any* number, Operator, *he* called *me!*"

SHE   "Your *call* did not go *through,* please hang *up* and dial *again.*"

HE   "But, Operator, I *can't* dial again."

SHE   "The *number* you have reached is *not* in service at this *time.*"

HE   "But I haven't *reached* any number, Operator!"

SHE   *"Please* check your directory and—"

HE   *"He* called *me,* don't you understand? *God* called *me!* He was *on the line!*"

SHE   "I'm *sorry,* your party doesn't seem to *answer."*

HE   "But he said he had GOOD NEWS and it was *very* important and to write it all down, and then all of a sudden the line just went *dead!* Do you hear me? I said *the line just went dead!* Hello? *Hello?"*

SHE   "The *time* at the *tone* will be *twelve* forty-*two."*

HE   "Oh boy!" said the man. "What a swell time for a *joke!"*

SHE   "Just a *mo*ment, I'll con*nect* you."

HE   "What do you *mean,* you'll connect me?"

SHE   "Hi, sport!" said another voice on the other end of the line. "I'm your local connection, how's *Life* treating you?"

HE   "Very funny," said the man. "Get *out* of my telephone; I'm looking for *God."*

54 | SHE   "Oh, golly, I'm just a poor Devil who lives all alone in a phonebooth. What's the GOOD NEWS?"

HE   "I'm *not* laughing."

SHE   "Well, consider the source. It's a *hell*uva joke, *isn't* it?"

HE   "For *your* information—"

SHE   *Burr-beep!* went a funny noise on the other end of the line.

HE   "Hello? Hello? Oh, boy," said the man. "Whatever happened to *good clean fun?"*

SHE   And just then the man noticed that he was still holding his mechanical pencil with the five colored leads and the blank pad of fifteen pages he had got out to write the GOOD NEWS on.

HE   And the man reflected on the inadequacies of Life

SHE   And the silence of God

HE   And the perversity of Information.

SHE   And all at once he was writing—

HE   A long, twisting sentence in red, yellow, blue, green, and black

SHE   That wandered back and forth through fifteen pages like a garden path through flower beds in full bloom

HE   Losing him at last among a blossomy profusion of great verbs and nouns with unfamiliar names and strange perfumes

SHE   Whose mingled fragrances he found so heady he might never have escaped at all

HE   Had not the magic garden withered unexpectedly on page fifteen when, luckily, his path ran off the paper at the bottom

SHE   And he wrote with great relief

HE   "And that is all the GOOD NEWS for today."

SHE   And he put his pencil down

HE   And stared at the telephone in a daze.

SHE   "Hello!" said a voice on the other end of the line

HE   So promptly the man had to wonder *who* had called *whom*.

SHE   "I'm your telephone company Service Representative."

HE   "Hello!" said the man. "I'm a man who lives all alone in a phonebooth!"

SHE   "Beautiful," said the Representative. "Did you lose your dime?"

HE   "No, I'm just starting an answering service, and *I'd* like to ask a few *questions*."

SHE   "What kind of answering service, sir?"

HE   "A *question* answering service."

SHE   "Under what *name?*"

HE   "I beg your pardon?"

SHE   "What is your *name?*"

HE   "Oh, yes," said the man. "Yes, my name."

SHE   And he had to stop and think for a moment because he wasn't at *all* sure he had one.

HE   And if he did, he *knew* it wasn't familiar.

SHE   "N-A-M-E," said the Service Representative. "What is your *nay-um?*"

HE   And the man looked down at the fifteen sheets of paper, covered with colorful language

SHE   And then over at the telephone

HE   And then up at the light in the phonebooth ceiling

SHE   Which *still* didn't' work

HE   And then *back* at the telephone again.

SHE   And then he shrugged his shoulders

HE   And took a deep breath

SHE   And made an irrevocable decision.

HE   "God," he said.

SHE   "I beg your pardon?"

HE   "It's my *business* name."

SHE   *"God's* Answering Service?"

HE   "Yes. May *I* be listed in the Yellow Pages?"

SHE   "Have you lost your marbles?"

HE   "I don't think so. It's pretty hard to lose *anything* in *here.*"

SHE   "Well, who are *you* but a man who lives all alone in a phonebooth?"

HE   "That's a *good question!*" said the man.

SHE   And in answer he read her all fifteen pages of the GOOD NEWS.

HE   "What do you think of *that?*"

SHE   "You've *lost* your marbles."

HE   "What makes you think so?"

SHE   *Click!* went the Service Representative's telephone.

HE   "Hello?" said the man. "Hello, hello?"

SHE   "Ha ha," said the voice of someone still on the line. *"Ha ha ha."*

HE   "You don't say!" said the man.

SHE   And he hung up and counted to ten

HE   "One, two, three four fivesixseveighni*ten!*"

SHE   And then picked up the receiver again.

HE   "Hello?"

SHE   *"Ha ha ha!"* came the laughter.

HE   There was more of it now.

SHE   Fifty voices maybe.

HE   Or a hundred. Or a *thousand!*

SHE   He could hear it getting louder and louder.

HE   "Listen!" he shouted. "What's so funny?"

SHE   *"Ha ha ha!"* came the answer. *"Ha ha ha ha ha!"* And suddenly the phonebooth was a *million* laughs.

HE   "My marbles," said the man, "are *not* where they used to be."

SHE   And he knew that *today* laughter had entered his life.

HE   "Well, let me *tell* you something!" he said. "Let me tell you! *I* don't mind being pestered by Life. *I* don't mind being cut off from God. I don't *even* mind getting the devil from Information."

SHE   *"Ha ha!"* laughed the million voices.

HE   "But it makes me *mad* to be *laughed* at!"

SHE   And indeed it did.

HE   For he promptly went out of his phonebooth and came undone

SHE   Stamping his bare feet and shouting loud, ugly, revolutionary slogans like

HE   "Information is a joke!"

SHE   And

HE   "Life is a dead issue!"

SHE   And

HE   "God is *not* a working number!"

SHE   In the process quickly killing

HE   Two hours

SHE   Any number of bottles

HE   A very difficult audience at the telephone company business office on West Ninety-third Street

SHE   And the entire front page of the next day's Daily News

HE   As well as his phone service *and* his chances in court

SHE   When telling his story to the cop on the corner

HE   He accidentally struck the policeman funny

SHE   And, taken into custody back to the station house

HE   Unwittingly caused the desk sergeant

SHE   The precinct captain

HE   Two detectives

SHE   And a lieutenant

HE   To knock themselves out in a back room

SHE   And die laughing.

HE   "Whatever happened to my marbles?" the man asked the judge.

SHE   In reply he was given a lengthy sentence

HE   In red, yellow, blue, green, and black

SHE   And a battered copy of the Life of his choice

HE   And never heard from again.

SHE   "Whatever happened to the man who lived all alone in the phonebooth?" people would say.

HE   No one knows

SHE   To this day.

HE   His *name* is not in the phone book.

SHE   And he has never called back to *say*.

HE   "Hello?"

BOTH [*Turning to each other*] "Hello?"

END

Noah Webster's Electrick Arktype

A Fable for Two Players

NOAH WEBSTER'S ELECTRICK ARKTYPE is an antiseman-
tic love song to that literary archetype of all civilized logic and order,
the Unabridged Dictionary, flagship of American rationality. (Well,
where else today can you still discover the true meaning of absolutely
everything?) My fable is about what happens when this linear, do-it-
yourself barge—heretofore undisputed ruler of the seas and loaded to
the gunwales with its regal, and heavily codified, cargo of law,
philosophy, and thrology—discovers it is not the only rowboat on the
ocean.

I wrote the first version (it ended with Noah's line: "That isn't land,
that's a pea green ark!") in the summer of 1967. The rest I added in
spurts during late 1971 and early 1972.

If you design costumes and props for this piece, I'd like to see
Noah dressed like a vaudeville version of Horatio Hornblower and
Alexia in correspondingly awful enlisted men's garb, both of them
sailing over the bounding main in a big, white, old-fashioned
bathtub afloat on cardboard waves, with one gray cardboard cloud
persistently overhead.

NOAH WEBSTER'S ELECTRICK ARKTYPE

*Aboard the good ship Ark. Noah is scanning the horizon through his
trusty glass, while his astigmatic wife Alexia rows.*

NOAH   Land ho!

ALEXIA   Oh, goodie, at last!

NOAH   What do you mean, at last?

ALEXIA   At last after forty days and forty nights you've sighted *land*.

NOAH   Are you kidding?

ALEXIA   Well, you said, "Land ho!" didn't you?

NOAH   Yes, but I was just *practicing*.

ALEXIA   Practicing?

NOAH   Every little bit helps.

ALEXIA   Try rowing!

NOAH   Don't be funny. I'm the captain. Captains don't row and you know it.

ALEXIA   Then why does the first mate always have to?

NOAH   Because the captain *says* so. The captain's word is law. It's a tradition on the high sea.

ALEXIA   This isn't the high sea, it's a flood.

NOAH   That's high enough.

ALEXIA   I don't see why *you* have to be the captain, anyway.

NOAH   The husband's *always* captain, it's a regulation.

ALEXIA   In whose navy?

NOAH   Mother Nature's.

ALEXIA   Mother Nature should turn in her naval button.

NOAH   Husbands are the captains, and the women are their mates. Women aren't the type to take command, you're not precise enough.

ALEXIA   We are *so*.

NOAH   Then how come every time I ask how long we've been

afloat, you tell me forty days and forty nights?

ALEXIA   What's wrong with that?

NOAH   You've been telling me that for *five months* now.

ALEXIA   It's a poetic metaphor.

NOAH   For what?

ALEXIA   For "long, long time."

NOAH   Very artistic.

ALEXIA   Metaphors are *always* true. Forty days and forty nights, it's got the right *sound.*

NOAH   Well, it's got the *wrong arithmetic!*

ALEXIA   Who notices but you?

NOAH   That's why I'm captain.

ALEXIA   Fooey!

NOAH   Anyway, I built this ark, *all* by myself.

ALEXIA   It looks it.

NOAH   While the rest of you laughed yourselves silly.

ALEXIA   It's a very funny ark.

NOAH   It's floating, isn't it?

ALEXIA   So far. But why in the world did you have to paint it fire engine red?

NOAH   Because I didn't happen to like pea green.

ALEXIA   *Pea green?*

NOAH   Yes, it takes a lot of paint to paint an ark, and the only other color the paint store had enough of was pea green.

ALEXIA   At least pea green would have been more natural.

NOAH   I don't hear the animals complaining.

ALEXIA   Who's complaining? It's dry!

NOAH   It certainly beats swimming.

ALEXIA   Not by much!

NOAH   Well, you don't know how it *hurt* me when you laughed.

ALEXIA   It hurt *me,* I haven't laughed that hard in years.

NOAH   *Most* wives wouldn't laugh like that at their *husbands.*

ALEXIA   *Most* wives wouldn't find their husbands trying to build an ark in the *firehouse basement.*

NOAH   That firehouse makes a dandy cabin.

ALEXIA   It's a big one, I'll say *that!*

NOAH   It's got a roof and four walls, hasn't it?

ALEXIA   Yeah, and a fire truck inside!

NOAH   I told you once a fire truck *may* come in handy.

ALEXIA   Well, who ever heard of an ark with a fire truck inside? For that matter, who ever heard of an *ark?*

NOAH   A *lot* of people. It's a common word used daily.

ALEXIA   In what language?

NOAH   In *our* language!

ALEXIA   Then how come *I* never heard of it?

NOAH   Because you never use your dictionary, that's why.

ALEXIA   Dictionaries bore me.

NOAH   Language is the passkey to the door of life.

ALEXIA In *my* book it's a blur.

NOAH   Put on your glasses.

ALEXIA I *broke* my glasses when you made me haul the *gangplank* in alone.

NOAH   Well, why were you wearing your glasses at a time like that?

ALEXIA I was looking up the meaning of *mutiny!*

NOAH   In *my* dictionary?

ALEXIA It was a *cheap thrill!*

NOAH   What'd you find?

ALEXIA A lot of small print.

NOAH   A precise vocabulary is the mark of a superior mind.

ALEXIA Baloney!

NOAH   Noun, a kind of sausage.

ALEXIA Not the way *I* say it!

NOAH   Listen, the way *you* say it is *not* a recognized meaning.

ALEXIA Everybody *I* know recognizes it.

NOAH   Well, it's *not* in the dictionary.

ALEXIA *Lots* of things aren't in the dictionary.

NOAH   How would *you* know?

ALEXIA Because I looked them up! Four letters and under I figured I could handle. I was furthering my education.

NOAH   With dirty words?

ALEXIA   With the book you gave me as a wedding present!

NOAH   Well, the dictionary is *not* a sex manual.

ALEXIA   You're telling *me!*

NOAH   There are more important things in life than sex.

ALEXIA   Name one.

NOAH   Scintillating conversation.

ALEXIA   Not on *this* scow, buddy!

NOAH   Well, it's not good business for the wife of a dictionary salesman to go around embarrassing everybody with her overblown lapsi linguae.

ALEXIA   Her what?

NOAH   Her *lapsi linguae.*

ALEXIA   Now *that* sounds *dirty!*

NOAH   If you don't know what it means, look it up.

ALEXIA   Look it up? I can't even spell it.

NOAH   A word a day will pave the way.

ALEXIA   Well, what's the word today?

NOAH   Row.

ALEXIA   Is that one law, too?

NOAH   They're all laws. Words are logical determinants of being.

ALEXIA   Well, I think I'd rather *be* something else.

NOAH   Believe me, you *are* something else!

ALEXIA   I mean besides first mate.

NOAH How about head keeper?

ALEXIA On a ship?

NOAH This isn't a ship, it's a floating zoo.

ALEXIA Well, what does the head keeper on a floating zoo *do?*

NOAH He keeps the head. What should he do?

ALEXIA Couldn't I be ship's doctor?

NOAH I don't know, can you treat worms?

ALEXIA What're they *sick* of?

NOAH Water, like everybody else. Just stick to rowing.

ALEXIA Any particular direction?

NOAH It's rower's choice.

ALEXIA How about straight down?

NOAH That's *not funny!* Especially in view of what happened last Saturday night.

ALEXIA I *always* take a tub bath on Saturday night.

NOAH Well, next time be careful which plug you pull!

ALEXIA I thought water ran out, not in.

NOAH *This* tub is different!

ALEXIA You can say *that* again.

NOAH But it's not supposed to be a submarine.

ALEXIA The water certainly was refreshing.

NOAH That reminds me, how're the animals?

ALEXIA They're looking weaker.

NOAH   Well, they're smelling stronger!

ALEXIA   You can't say they haven't had a bath.

NOAH   There's nothing like the smell of a damp elephant!

ALEXIA   We ran out of paper towels.

NOAH   We should have brought more supplies.

ALEXIA   We should have brought fewer *animals!* I had a feeling two by two equalled more than four.

NOAH   Well, you know what it says on the side of the ship.

ALEXIA   Yeah, "Noah Webster's."

NOAH   I mean down below that.

ALEXIA   "Unabridged."

NOAH   We take in everything.

ALEXIA   What happened to the human race then?

NOAH   I said *every*thing, not *any*thing. We *are* the human race.

ALEXIA   I meant the *rest* of it.

NOAH   They missed the boat, as usual.

ALEXIA   Well, it sure is scary floating around in circles out here all alone in the middle of nowhere with all these animals.

NOAH   That's the human predicament.

ALEXIA   Well, just remember—we wouldn't be *in* this predicament if you hadn't turned that silly fire hydrant on.

NOAH   I was only obeying orders.

ALEXIA   Orders?

NOAH   Yes, the world was on fire, and I was told to put it out.

ALEXIA   By whom?

NOAH   It's a secret.

ALEXIA   What do you mean, it's a secret?

NOAH   I mean you wouldn't believe me if I told you.

ALEXIA   Yes, I would. Who was it?

NOAH   God.

ALEXIA   I don't believe you! Where did *you* see *God*?

NOAH   On television, it was a special!

ALEXIA   It *must* have been special, *I* didn't see it.

NOAH   You were asleep. I woke up in the middle of the night, and there he was in living color saying, "The *world* is going up in *flames!* The *world* is going up in *flames!*"

ALEXIA   On television?

NOAH   Yes, and I don't think the set was even turned on.

ALEXIA   Well, *you* certainly must have been!

NOAH   Men see things that women don't.

ALEXIA   I'll say, what was on fire? I didn't even see flames!

NOAH   The soul of man was burning.

ALEXIA   That would be hard to see!

NOAH   The imagination of his heart was as a consuming fire, and the words of his mouth as unquenchable tongues of flame. The world was ablaze with confusion.

ALEXIA   Did God say that?

NOAH   His very words.

ALEXIA   Thank goodness you heard the alarm.

NOAH   He said the framework of human existence was burning down and wouldn't somebody kindly put it out. So I got up and told him, "Here am I; send me, send me."

ALEXIA   And what did God say?

NOAH   "Turn the fire hydrant on and run!"

ALEXIA   But what about the ark?

NOAH   I asked him where in the world to run *to,* and he said that was a *very* good question.

ALEXIA   And gave you the plans.

NOAH   No, he just said it was a good question. Then he went into a commercial, and I fell asleep.

ALEXIA   You volunteer firemen are all alike.

NOAH   Actually the ark was my *own* idea.

ALEXIA   That certainly restores my faith in God.

NOAH   The righteous have finally inherited the earth.

ALEXIA   The righteous?

NOAH   The pure in speech.

ALEXIA   I thought the meek were supposed to inherit it.

NOAH   The meek talked funny.

ALEXIA   Well, as far as I can see, all *anybody's* going to inherit so far is a lot of dirty, polluted water.

NOAH   It's the ark that's important.

ALEXIA   Some inheritance!

NOAH   A tiny speck of meaning on a sea of nothingness. The

good ship truth afloat upon the void! That's how I *see* it.

ALEXIA   You certainly have grown fond of the idea.

NOAH   It's a lexicographer's *dream*.

ALEXIA   A *who?*

NOAH   A lexicographer, someone who handles morphemes.

ALEXIA   I thought that was a pusher.

NOAH   A morpheme is a particle of meaning.

ALEXIA   Well, it sounds habit-forming.

NOAH   It's what *words* are made of.

ALEXIA   I thought words were made of *sounds*.

NOAH   When they're grammatical, they're morphemes.

ALEXIA   Let's forget it.

NOAH   Logical organization is important.

ALEXIA   It's neurotic, if you ask me.

NOAH   Civilization stays afloat on inventoried morphemes.

ALEXIA   Well, I still think making the animals come up the plank in alphabetical order was going a little too far!

NOAH   Those animals needed analysis.

ALEXIA   I think *you* needed analysis!

NOAH   Alphabetical arrangement helps to order chaos.

ALEXIA   Well, it certainly confused the dodo and the dinosaur.

NOAH   What's the matter with *them?*

ALEXIA   They both jumped overboard this morning.

NOAH   Whatever *for?*

ALEXIA   They said they couldn't stand it in adjoining staterooms. The dinosaur said he felt alphabetical order was unnatural, and the dodo said yes, it was no wonder everyone always called humans dumb.

NOAH   The dodo shouldn't talk!

ALEXIA   So they both jumped overboard.

NOAH   Together?

ALEXIA   Not exactly. The dinosaur said he'd sooner swim, and the dodo said she'd rather go by air.

NOAH   But they can't *do* that!

ALEXIA   That's what they discovered.

NOAH   Well, I hope they learned their lesson.

ALEXIA   They seemed to. Last I saw they had their arms around each other like old friends.

NOAH   Fine. Where were they going?

ALEXIA   Down! For the third time. You can't say they weren't spunky.

NOAH   Well, frankly, they both struck me as being just a little bit odd. As far as I'm concerned, it's just two less mouths to feed. And as I remember, they were pretty big mouths.

ALEXIA   They certainly were.

NOAH   That reminds me, isn't it feeding time?

ALEXIA   Yes, it is.

NOAH   Then why aren't you feeding the animals?

ALEXIA   I thought I ought to ask you something first.

NOAH   What's that?

ALEXIA   What do we do when we run out of food?

NOAH   What makes you ask?

ALEXIA   We just ran out of food!

NOAH   Well, you did the figuring. What's the problem?

ALEXIA   Multiplication.

NOAH   Multiplication?

ALEXIA   One-and-one-makes-three.

NOAH   Are you kidding?

ALEXIA   Anywhere from three to a dozen.

NOAH   *That's* no way to *multiply*.

ALEXIA   Try telling that to the rabbits!

NOAH   Since when are the rabbits doing arithmetic?

ALEXIA   Believe me, what those rabbits are doing I *wouldn't* call arithmetic.

NOAH   Well, what would you call it?

ALEXIA   A big *mistake!*

NOAH   Don't be silly. Itty-bitty rabbits don't make big mistakes.

ALEXIA   Oh, no?

NOAH   Just lots of little ones.

ALEXIA   *That's* what seems to be the *problem.*

NOAH   Well, the rabbits don't seem to think it's a problem.

ALEXIA   Wait'll they stop long enough to eat.

NOAH   I think you're out of luck.

ALEXIA   *They're* out of luck. *I'm* out of *rabbit food.*

NOAH   Well, what can we do?

ALEXIA   How does feeding them to the lions sound to you?

NOAH   Will it help the rabbits?

ALEXIA   It won't hurt the lions any.

NOAH   Are we out of lion food, too?

ALEXIA   Not until we're out of rabbits.

NOAH   But is that moral?

ALEXIA   It depends on whether you're a rabbit or a lion. When I
          mentioned it to the lions, they went wild.

NOAH   What did the rabbits say?

ALEXIA   I'd hate to tell you.

NOAH   Rabbits have a one-track mind.

ALEXIA   I told them flattery would get them nowhere.

NOAH   Good girl.

ALEXIA   After all, this is an emergency. Starvation is no picnic.
          We've got to do *something.*

NOAH   Yes, maybe we should start looking for land again.

ALEXIA   Land, are you kidding? I'm blind without my glasses.

NOAH   Well, just keep your eyes open for something that's not
          water.

ALEXIA   Anything?

NOAH   At this point we can't afford to be choosey.

ALEXIA   Well, how about that little dark spot over there on the horizon?

NOAH   Humnh?

ALEXIA   That funny little thing with the flag.

NOAH   Where?

ALEXIA   There, dead ahead.

NOAH   [*Using his glass*] With the animals on it?

ALEXIA   Yes, and that luscious green grass.

NOAH   Good gracious!

ALEXIA   Should I shout, "Land ho"?

NOAH   I think you better yell, "Fire!"

ALEXIA   Fire?

NOAH   That isn't land, that's a pea green ark!

ALEXIA   A pea green ark?

NOAH   With a big neon sign on it.

ALEXIA   What does it say?

NOAH   [*Reading it through his glass*] "Truth never changes, but definitions do."

ALEXIA   It's amazing what a little electric power'll do to people.

NOAH   [*His eye still glued to the glass*] You don't know the half of it. The aardvark's got his arm around the zebra, and the buffalo's kissing the yak on the poop deck.

ALEXIA   It sounds like a pretty fast ship.

NOAH   It's frightening.

ALEXIA   Where're they headed?

NOAH   Straight at us, that's what's frightening.

ALEXIA   Gee, I wonder how they're fixed for rabbits.

NOAH   In a minute you can ask them.

ALEXIA   You mean we'll be hailing them?

NOAH   No, hitting them. We're on a collision course.

ALEXIA   Maybe they don't see us.

NOAH   Are you kidding? The whole boatload's lined up at the rail with binoculars.

ALEXIA   Well, that doesn't prove they see us.

NOAH   And the way they're all laughing, you'd think they never looked at anything so funny in their lives.

ALEXIA   They see us. [*She starts rowing.*]

NOAH   One silly ape with a red hat and a hose is even jumping up and down on the bridge, pointing.

ALEXIA   Wouldn't you know! A whole *world* full of water, and *we* run into another volunteer fireman.

NOAH   Well, if he thinks he scares *me,* he's in for a big surprise.

ALEXIA   What are your orders?

NOAH   Full speed astern!

ALEXIA   [*Rowing hard*] I'm *going* full speed astern.

NOAH   Then how come we're still moving forward?

ALEXIA   We're caught in the current.

NOAH   *What* current?

ALEXIA   I'd tell you the name, but I can't figure out where we are.

NOAH   We're *up the creek! That's* where we are.

ALEXIA   [*She stops rowing.*] I'll check the atlas.

NOAH   For*get* it! Just get out the signal book and prepare to send a message.

ALEXIA   To whom?

NOAH   To the ape at the wheel of that unripe banana boat.

ALEXIA   [*Getting out a huge volume*] What should I say?

NOAH   *Stop!*

ALEXIA   That's a very good start. [*Consulting her book, she wigwags the message.*]

NOAH   Out of control stop. Caught in the current stop. Can't stop stop.

ALEXIA   Um?

NOAH   Can't *stop* stop!

ALEXIA   O*kay*kay!

NOAH   Change course at once stop. That is an order stop.

ALEXIA   Right. Is that all?

NOAH   No, RSVP.

ALEXIA   *RSVP?*

NOAH   I like to be polite.

ALEXIA   To an *ape?*

NOAH   Listen, he may be on the market for a dictionary. Look, he's sending back a message already.

ALEXIA   [*Squinting hard*] What's he saying?

NOAH   "Stop."

ALEXIA   It sounds vaguely familiar.

NOAH   "Out of control stop. Caught in the current stop. Can't stop stop. Change course at once stop. That is an order stop."

ALEXIA   That's the whole message?

NOAH   No, "RSVP."

ALEXIA   You're sure you're not looking in a mirror?

NOAH   Maybe you'd better send another message.

ALEXIA   Well, make it short or I'll be sending it underwater.

NOAH   Right. Now hear this.

ALEXIA   That's more like it. [*She sends it.*]

NOAH   This flood protected by copyright.

ALEXIA   Now you're telling him.

NOAH   Your unauthorized use of this material punishable by law.

ALEXIA   Lay it on thick.

NOAH   Scuttle your vessel, and go down with your ship immediately.

ALEXIA   How should I sign the message?

NOAH   The Admiral.

ALEXIA   The Admiral?

NOAH   I've just had another religious experience.

ALEXIA   I hope it works better than the last one. [*Having finished signaling, she is closing her eyes, putting her fingers in her*